11/17

First Facts®

CURIOUS SCIENTISTS

EYE-OPENING EARTH SCIENCE ACTIVITIES

by Rani Iyer

CAPSTONE PRESS
a capstone imprint

First Facts are published by Capstone Press,
1710 Roe Crest Drive, North Mankato, Minnesota 56003
www.mycapstone.com

Library of Congress Cataloging-in-Publication Data
Cataloging-in-publication information is on file with the Library of Congress.
ISBN 978-1-5157-6885-2 (library binding)
ISBN 978-1-5157-6891-3 (paperback)
ISBN 978-1-5157-6903-3 (eBook PDF)

Editorial Credits
Anna Butzer, editor; Heidi Thompson, designer; Morgan Walters, media researcher; Kathy McColley, production specialist

Photo Credits
All photos are shot by the Capstone Studio, Karon Dubke

Artistic Elements
Shutterstock: amgun, (gears) design element throughout

Printed and bound in the USA.
010374F17

TABLE OF CONTENTS

DIGGING DEEP

Do you often wonder how the world around you works? When you visit your favorite beach, do you wonder why it looks different than the last time you saw it? On a cloudy day, do you ask yourself how clouds form? To find out the answers to questions like these, curious scientists do experiments.

Now it's your turn to be a curious scientist. Get ready to use your creativity and get a little messy! You will learn about the rock cycle, cool cave formations, and more. The results will be eye opening!

Safe Science

Read through each activity before starting. Collect all of the materials that you will need. You may need an adult to help you find or buy some materials. Experiments can be tricky. Be sure to ask an adult for help if you need it.

CLOUD IN A JAR

To some people a cloudy sky means a ruined day at the beach, but clouds are an important part of Earth's weather. Clouds are made up of tiny water droplets and ice crystals that are so small they float in the air. Learn how these droplets form and make your own cloud in a jar!

Materials:

- jar with a lid
- 1/2 cup (118 milliliters) very hot water
- ice cubes
- hairspray

Steps:

1. Ask an adult to help you pour the hot water into the jar.
2. Turn the lid upside down and place it on top of the jar.
3. Put a handful of ice cubes on top. Let the ice cubes sit there for 15-20 seconds.
4. Remove the lid and spray a bit of hairspray into the jar.
5. Quickly replace the lid with the ice still on top. Watch the cloud form inside the jar!

How it Works:

Three things are needed to make a cloud: moist air, cooling, and small particles for water **vapors** to **condense** onto. When the hot water is added to the jar some of it turns to water vapor. The vapor rises to the top of the jar. It comes in contact with the cold air caused by the ice cubes. In nature, water vapor may condense onto things such as dust particles, pollen, or air pollution. In this activity, the water vapor condensed onto the hairspray. That is why you see a cloud form in the jar!

vapor—a gas made from something that is usually a liquid or solid at normal temperatures

condense—to change from a gas to a liquid: water vapor condenses into liquid water

CRAYON ROCK CYCLE

Have you ever wondered why some rocks are broken up into small pieces and others are round and smooth? Have you seen rocks that look like they are made up of different layers? Use crayons to learn about the rock cycle! Crayons can be heated, **compressed**, and cooled to help us better understand the three types of rocks that make up the rock cycle. These types of rocks are **sedimentary**, **metamorphic**, and **igneous rocks**.

Materials:

- 2–3 different colored wax crayons, papers removed
- handheld pencil sharpener or plastic knife
- aluminum foil or foil cupcake liners
- source of hot water
- container to hold hot water

Steps:

1. Use a sharpener or plastic knife to shave the crayons into small pieces. Keep the different colors separate.

Step 1

8

2. Sprinkle a layer of each color crayon onto a piece of aluminum foil. This represents the laying down of sediments.

3. Fold up the foil and press down on it very hard. This is an example of the pressure that creates sedimentary rock. Unwrap the foil and examine your first crayon rock.

Step 4

4. Ask an adult to pour hot water into a bowl. Rewrap your crayon rock from step 3 in foil and dunk it in the water for 15-20 seconds.

compress—to squeeze together into less space

sedimentary rock—rock formed by layers of rocks, sand, or clay that have been pressed together

metamorphic rock—rock that is changed by heat and pressure

igneous rock—rock that forms when magma, melted rock found beneath Earth's surface, cools

5. Carefully pull it out of the water and gently squish it a bit more. Let it cool and solidify. Open the foil and remove and examine the second crayon rock in the cycle.

Step 5

6. For the last type of rock in the rock cycle, ask an adult to heat up more water. Rewrap your crayon rock in foil and dunk it in the water. This time you'll need to leave it in the hot water for a minute or longer. All of the crayon shavings need to melt.

7. Take the foil out of the water and let the crayon cool and solidify.

Your crayons have gone through a cycle similar to the rock cycle. The crayons start off smooth and hard. Then they are broken into smaller pieces and stuck together again in layers. After being melted together and cooled a couple times they feel smooth and hard again.

How it Works:

Sedimentary rocks are formed from sediments that are layered and then pressed together. You made a sedimentary rock when you layered the different crayon shavings on top of each other and squished them together. Metamorphic rocks are formed when existing rocks are exposed to heat and pressure. You created a metamorphic rock by putting your sedimentary rock in the hot water for 15 seconds. Igneous rocks form when melted rock found beneath the surface of the earth called magma cools. To make the crayon wax melt, you had to leave the metamorphic rock in the hot water longer. After it cooled and solidified you had an igneous rock. The rock cycle is never ending!

STALACTITES AND STALAGMITES

Stalactites and stalagmites can be found in caves around the world. Stalactites grow down from cave ceilings and stalagmites grow up from the cave floor. They grow at a very slow rate — about 1 inch (2.5 cm) a year! Make your own cave formations faster with this activity.

Materials:

- 2 identical glasses or jars
- very warm water
- bowl
- Epsom salts
- spoon
- small plate
- string
- scissors
- 2 small weights (washers, paperclips, etc.)

Steps:

1. Fill the glasses or jars with warm water all the way to the top. Pour the water into a large bowl.
2. Start adding the Epsom salts to the bowl. Stir to dissolve. Keep adding salts and stirring until no more salt will dissolve. Warmer water will be able to dissolve more salt.
3. Carefully divide the solution into the two glasses. Place them aside where they won't be disturbed. Set the plate in between the glasses.

4. Cut the string. It should be long enough to reach the bottom of both glasses.
5. Put a small weight on each end of the string. Put one end of the string in each of the glasses. There should be a small dip in the middle of the string.
6. Check on your stalactites and stalagmites every day. Give them a few days to form.

How it Works:

The Epsom salt mix is carried through the string and drips onto the plate. Over time, the dripping water evaporates, and a mini stalactite and stalagmite are formed. Real stalactites and stalagmites are formed in almost the same way.

Most stalactites and stalagmites are found in limestone caves. The rocks in these caves contain a mineral called calcite. When it rains, water trickles through the cracks in the cave rocks. The calcite-rich water dripping from the cave ceiling forms the stalactite. The water drips down from the end of the stalactite and falls to the cave floor. This is why you usually see stalactites and stalagmites in pairs. Sometimes they'll even connect and grow together, forming a column.

WATER EROSION

Have you heard of the Grand Canyon? It is so big and deep it can be seen from space! It took millions of years to form. But how did something so great happen? Erosion!

Materials:

- rectangular aluminum roasting or cake pan
- sand
- water
- six marbles or small rocks
- plastic spoon

Steps:

1. Pour the sand into one end of the pan. The walls of your pan should be at least 3 inches (7.6 cm) high.
2. Slowly pour about 1 inch (2.5 cm) of water into the pan. Make sure to pour at the end opposite of the sand.

Step 2

3. Place six marbles or rocks on the sand above the water. Put them in different places to act as markers.

4. Use the spoon and slowly start making small waves.

5. Did the marbles move? What changes did you notice in the shoreline?

How it Works:

Water is the main cause of erosion on Earth. Water erosion comes in different forms, including rainfall, rivers, floods, and more. The result of this activity is similar to what happens at the beach. Waves constantly crash against the shore. Water erosion changes the shape of coastlines. Ocean waves take sand away from beaches and erode seaside cliffs.

EGG GEODE

In a crystal, **matter** is arranged in an orderly form. Geodes are crystals that form deep in the Earth. In this activity, you will learn how to make an egg geode.

Materials:

- 1 egg
- paper towels
- PVA glue
- paintbrush
- alum powder
- 2 cups (470 ml) very hot water
- spoon
- liquid measuring glass
- 2 glasses
- food color or egg dye

Steps:

1. Carefully crack the egg in half. Rinse the inside out with warm water.
2. Remove the inside membrane and any loose pieces from the shell with your fingers.
3. Use a paper towel to dry the inside of the egg.
4. Pour some glue into both halves of the eggshell. Use the paintbrush to coat the inside of the shells and the edges with the glue.

Step 1

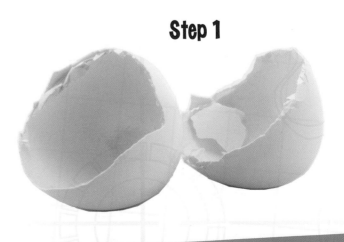

matter—anything that has weight and takes up space

5. Generously sprinkle alum powder on any surface covered with glue. Tap off the excess powder. Let the eggshells sit out overnight to dry.

6. Ask an adult to help you fill a liquid measuring glass with two cups of hot water. Add ¾ cup (133 grams) of alum powder to the hot water. Stir until the powder is completely dissolved. Let it cool for about 20 minutes.

Step 5

7. Divide the water equally into two glasses and add the food coloring. Put about 15 to 20 drops into each glass.
8. Set an eggshell half in each glass. Make sure the alum-coated side is facing up. Use a spoon to carefully push the shells all the way to the bottom of the glass.
9. Wait 12 to 15 hours before removing the eggshells. Carefully remove the shells and let them dry completely.

Tip: The longer the eggshells are in the solution, the larger the crystal geodes will be!

Step 8

How it Works:

These eggshell geodes form through a process called **sedimentation**. A geological geode is a hollow rock that is lined with minerals. Real geodes take millions of years to form, but our egg geodes only took a couple of days. The heated water has tiny pieces of alum floating in it. As the water cools, the alum starts falling to the bottom and begins crystallizing. The alum coated shell gives the floating pieces a place where they can attach themselves. They crystallize quickly, creating an amazing egg geode!

sedimentation—the process in which particles suspended in water to sink to the bottom

SEEING SOLAR ENERGY

The sun gives us a lot of energy in the form of heat. This experiment will show you how to collect the sun's, or solar, energy as heat.

Materials:

- two clear plastic 2-liter bottles, empty
- black and white craft paint
- paintbrush
- two balloons

Steps:

1. Paint both of the bottles, one white and one black. Let the paint dry.
2. Attach a balloon to the top of each bottle.
3. Place both bottles somewhere they will be exposed to sunlight.
4. Watch what happens. Which balloon inflates more?

How it Works:

   The energy we get from the sun is very important. It warms our planet. The sun heats Earth's surface, the oceans, and the atmosphere. The sun gives energy to the Earth in the form of **radiation**. For example, as the sun's radiation heats the ground, the ground heats up and releases heat into the air. The warm air then rises.

   When the sun shines on an object, the object can reflect light or absorb it. The color white reflects light while the color black absorbs it. The light being absorbed converts to heat energy. This energy heats up the bottle and causes it and the balloon to expand.

GLOSSARY

compress (KAHM-pres)—to squeeze together into less space

condense (kuhn-DENS)—to change from gas to liquid; water vapor condenses into liquid water

igneous rock (IG-nee-uhss ROK)—rock that forms when magma cools

matter (MAT-ur)—anything that has weight and takes up space

metamorphic rock (met-uh-MOR-fik ROK)—rock that is changed by heat and pressure

radiation (ray-dee-AY-shuhn)—rays of energy given off by certain elements

sedimentary rock (sed-uh-MEN-tuh-ree ROK)—rock formed by layers of rocks, sand, or clay that have been pressed together

sedimentation (sed-uh-muhn-TAY-shuhn)—the process in which particles suspended in water to sink to the bottom

READ MORE

Gardner, Robert. *Science Fair Projects about Planet Earth*. Hands-on Science. New York: Enslow Publishing, 2017.

Sohn, Emily. *Experiments in Earth Science and Weather with Toys and Everyday Stuff*. Fun Science. North Mankato, Minn.: Capstone Press, 2015.

Thomas, Isabel. *Experiments with Heating and Cooling*. Read and Experiment. Chicago: Heinemann Raintree, 2015.

INTERNET SITES

Use FactHound to find Internet sites related to this book.

Visit *www.facthound.com*

Just type in 9781515768852 and go.

Check out projects, games and lots more at **www.capstonekids.com**

INDEX